SO-AZJ-536

Saturn

Uranus

Neptune

NOV   4/ 2008
MUNDY BRANCH
Onondaga County
Public Library
1204 S GEDDES STREET
SYRACUSE NY 13204

Galaxies and the Universe

Editor in chief: Paul A. Kobasa
Supplementary Publications: Jeff De La Rosa, Lisa Kwon,
    Christine Sullivan, Scott Thomas, Marty Zwikel
Research: Mike Barr, Cheryl Graham, Jacqueline Jasek,
    Barbara Lightner, Andy Roberts, Loranne Shields
Graphics and Design: Kathy Creech, Sandra Dyrlund,
    Charlene Epple, Tom Evans, Brenda Tropinski
Permissions: Janet Peterson
Indexing: David Pofelski
Pre-Press and Manufacturing: Carma Fazio, Anne Fritzinger,
    Steven Hueppchen, Tina Ramirez
Writer: Dan Blunk

© 2007 World Book, Inc. All rights reserved. This book may not
be reproduced in whole or in part in any form without prior
written permission from the publisher.

First edition published 2006. Second edition published 2007.

WORLD BOOK and the GLOBE DEVICE are registered
trademarks or trademarks of World Book, Inc.

World Book, Inc.
233 N. Michigan Avenue
Chicago, IL 60601
U.S.A.

Library of Congress Cataloging-in-Publication Data
Galaxies and the universe. -- 2nd ed.
    p. cm. --(World Book's solar system & space exploration
library)
    Includes bibliographical references and index.
    Summary: "Introduction to Galaxies and the Universe,
providing to primary and intermediate grade students,
information on their features and exploration. Includes fun
facts, glossary, resource list and index"--Provided by publisher.
    ISBN-13: 978-0-7166-9513-4
    ISBN-10: 0-7166-9513-8
    1. Galaxies--Juvenile literature. 2. Astronomy--Juvenile
literature. 3. Solar system--Juvenile literature. I. World Book,
Inc.
QB857.3.G35 2007
523.1'12--dc22
                            2006030040

ISBN-13 (set): 978-0-7166-9511-0
ISBN-10 (set): 0-7166-9511-1

Printed in the United States of America

1 2 3 4 5 6 7 8 09 08 07 06

**For information about other World Book publications,
visit our Web site at http://www.worldbook.com
or call 1-800-WORLDBK (967-5325).**

**For information about sales to schools and libraries,
call 1-800-975-3250 (United States);
1-800-837-5365 (Canada).**

Picture Acknowledgments: Front Cover: © David A. Hardy, Futures: 50 Years In Space/SPL/Photo
Researchers; Back Cover: NASA; NASA/ESA/STScI/AURA; © Margaret Bourke-White, Time & Life
Pictures/Getty Images; NOAO/AURA/NSF 21; Inside Back Cover: © John Gleason, Celestial Images.

© John Gleason, Celestial Images 10, 11; ESA 53; ESO 7; © Margaret Bourke-White, Time & Life
Pictures/Getty Images 39; Myungkook James Jee, Johns Hopkins University 51; NASA 15, 43, 47, 61 (inset);
NASA/CXC/MIT 25; NASA/CXC/SAO 57; NASA/ESA 19, 61; NASA/GSFC/NOAA/NGDC 31; NASA/JHU 45;
NASA/JHU/The Hebrew Univ./STScI/UCO/Lick Observatory/ACS Science; Team/ESA 59; NASA/PSU 49;
NASA/STScI/AURA 1, 9, 23, 29, 41, 55; NASA/STScI/AURA/ESA 27, 37; NASA/STScI/ESA/HUDF 33; NOAO
35; NOAO/AURA/NSF 21; © Mark Garlick, SPL/Photo Researchers 13; © David A. Hardy, Futures: 50 Years
In Space/SPL/Photo Researchers 3, 17.

Illustrations: Inside Front Cover: WORLD BOOK illustration by Steve Karp; WORLD BOOK illustration by
Charlene Epple 40.

Astronomers use different kinds of photos to learn about objects in space—such as planets. Many photos
show an object's natural color. Other photos use false colors. Some false-color images show types of light the
human eye cannot normally see. Others have colors that were changed to highlight important features. When
appropriate, the captions in this book state whether a photo uses natural or false color.

WORLD BOOK'S

SOLAR SYSTEM & SPACE EXPLORATION LIBRARY

Galaxies and the Universe

SECOND EDITION

World Book, Inc.
a Scott Fetzer company
Chicago

Contents

GALAXIES

If a word is printed in **bold letters that look like this,** that word's meaning is given in the glossary on page 63.

THE UNIVERSE

What Is a Galaxy?

A **galaxy** is a collection of gas, dust, and millions or even billions of stars, which is held together by **gravity.** A good way to think of a galaxy is as an island of **matter** in the vast emptiness of outer space.

Galaxies are huge. Some are far more than 100,000 **light-years** across.

After years of discovering and studying galaxies, **astronomers** have learned that galaxies come in many shapes and sizes, and that no two are exactly alike.

A spiral galaxy in a false-color composite image

What Are Galaxies Made Of?

Galaxies contain large numbers of stars. **Astronomers** and other scientists first discovered and learned about galaxies by observing the light from the stars. But galaxies are made of much more than stars. They also contain such things as **planets, asteroids,** and huge clouds of gas and dust. All of these objects in space have one thing in common—they are made of a type of **matter** that is visible (that can be seen). Matter is visible because it either gives off or reflects light.

Galaxies also contain another type of matter that is much different from that which makes up stars, planets, and other objects in space. This type of matter is called **dark matter,** because it does not give off or reflect light and so cannot be seen with a telescope. Dark matter is invisible, but scientists think it makes up most of the **mass** in the **universe.** Although they cannot see dark matter, scientists know it is there because they have detected the effects of its **gravity** on other objects.

The Sombrero Galaxy
in a natural-color
composite image

What Galaxy Are We In?

Our **solar system,** which includes the sun, Earth, and the other **planets** in **orbit** around our sun, is located in a **galaxy** called the Milky Way. The Milky Way contains hundreds of billions of other stars besides our sun, as well as huge clouds of dust and gas.

On a dark night, distant parts of the Milky Way can be seen from Earth. The individual stars in some regions are

too far away to be seen unaided. But the light the stars give off can be seen as a white haze that looks like spilled milk. Ancient people looking up at the sky noticed this and gave our galaxy its name before anyone knew what it was!

The Milky Way Galaxy in a natural-color photo

What Is the Shape of the Milky Way Galaxy?

The Milky Way is in the shape of a **spiral.** Spiral **galaxies** are shaped like disks, with a bulge in the center and "arms" that swirl outward in a spiral, or coiled, shape. If you were standing directly above the Milky Way looking down at it, it would look somewhat like a pinwheel.

The arms that curve outward from the center of a spiral galaxy consist of stars and other **matter,** such as gas and dust. Many of the oldest stars in the Milky Way are in the central bulge. The younger stars are in the spiral arms, away from the center of the galaxy.

An artist's conception
of the Milky Way Galaxy

How Big Is the Milky Way?

The Milky Way is enormous. In one year, light travels about 5.88 trillion miles—that is, 5.88 million million miles (9.46 trillion kilometers). If you could travel at the **speed of light,** it would take you 100,000 years to get from one end of the Milky Way to the other!

The Milky Way is so massive that there are many smaller **galaxies** in **orbit** around it, like **satellites** orbiting a **planet.** Not only is the Milky Way huge from end to end, its disk is also almost 2,000 **light-years** thick. The central bulge is many times thicker. The Milky Way has so much **matter** that scientists estimate that our galaxy contains about 200 billion stars.

Though the Milky Way is so large, galaxies can be even larger. The most massive galaxies can have 100 times more mass—in the form of stars, hot gas, and other matter—than the Milky Way.

The Milky Way Galaxy viewed from the side, in an infrared image

Where Is Our Solar System in the Milky Way?

People who lived long ago thought that our **planet** was at the center of everything. They thought all the other planets, and even the sun, revolved around Earth. Today, we know that Earth is not at the center of the **solar system** or our **galaxy.**

Our solar system is actually located in one of the outer arms of the Milky Way. This arm is called the Orion arm. Earth is very far—about 25,000 **light-years**—from the center of the galaxy. In Earth's part of the galaxy stars are, on average, about five light-years away from each other. Nearer to the center of the galaxy stars are about 100 times closer to each other. For this reason, the center of the galaxy appears extremely bright.

Artist's drawings showing the location of our solar system in the Milky Way Galaxy

Our solar system

The Milky Way Galaxy viewed from above

Our solar system

The Milky Way Galaxy viewed from the side

How Did Our Solar System Form in the Milky Way?

Scientists believe that about five billion years ago our **solar system** was just a giant, rotating cloud of dust and gas inside the Milky Way **Galaxy.** Then, this cloud began to collapse under the pull of **gravity.** Some scientists think that a nearby **supernova** triggered the collapse. As the cloud collapsed, the gas and dust began to spin faster and flatten out, becoming a large disk of **matter.**

The disk continued to collapse under its own weight and to draw in more gas and dust. At the center of the disk, the gravity was so strong and the particles (pieces) were pulled so closely together that the pressure was tremendous. This pressure was so great that it triggered the **nuclear fusion reactions** that caused the sun to begin shining as a star.

In a similar way, fragments of rock in the disk combined to create the inner **planets**—Mercury, Venus, Earth, and Mars. Gases, dust, and ice farther from the sun collected to form the **gas giants,** including Jupiter and Saturn. According to this theory, **asteroids** and **comets** are made of material that was left over from the formation of the solar system.

supernova

A supernova exploding in a distant galaxy, in a false-color image

What Is the Milky Way's Neighborhood Like?

The Milky Way is part of the Local Group, a collection of galaxies that includes our own **galaxy** and more than 30 relatively nearby galaxies. Two of these nearby galaxies—Andromeda *(an DROM uh duh)* and M33—are large **spiral** galaxies like the Milky Way. The Local Group also contains two famous galaxies called the Large Magellanic *(MAJ uh LAN ihk)* Cloud and the Small Magellanic Cloud, which are visible from Earth.

The large cluster of galaxies nearest to the Local Group is called the Virgo Cluster. This cluster is named after the **constellation** Virgo. Virgo is located in the Milky Way Galaxy, but the constellation can be seen in the same part of Earth's night sky as the galaxies that form the Virgo Cluster.

The Local Group and the Virgo Cluster are part of an even larger group of galaxies called a supercluster. The supercluster these galaxies are in is called the Local Supercluster. Scientists have discovered that superclusters are arranged in chains, with huge empty spaces in between them where no galaxies exist.

The Andromeda Galaxy in a natural-color composite photo

How Did Galaxies Form?

Scientists have developed two main theories to explain how **galaxies** formed. In one theory, small structures such as globular clusters (groups of tens of thousands to a few million stars) formed first. Then, galaxies and galaxy clusters formed as many smaller groups of stars moved closer together. The other theory states that larger structures, such as galaxies and galaxy clusters, formed first, and that globular clusters formed within them afterward.

Despite the obvious differences between these theories, they both agree that shortly after the **universe** began, **matter** started to collect more heavily in some areas than in others. As more matter joined these matter-heavy areas, they began to spin and grow larger, eventually becoming globular clusters, galaxies, and galaxy clusters—but not necessarily in that order.

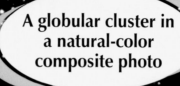

A globular cluster in a natural-color composite photo

Does the Milky Way Travel in an Orbit?

The Milky Way is similar to our own **solar system** in that it is constantly in motion. In much the same way that **planets** are in **orbit** around the sun, the clusters of stars and other objects in the Milky Way orbit around the center of the **galaxy.**

Because the Milky Way is so huge, it takes the sun about 250 million years to complete one orbit around the galactic center! Other stars may take more or less time to complete an orbit, depending on how far they are from the center. Some objects, such as certain dust clouds, take much longer to complete their orbit around the galaxy's center.

Astronomers have studied the orbit of the stars in the Milky Way using powerful **instruments,** which include telescopes that detect radio waves—a type of **electromagnetic energy.** These scientists have determined that everything in the Milky Way is orbiting around a small object with a huge amount of **mass** in the exact center of the galaxy. Scientists believe this object, called Sagittarius *(SAJ uh TAIR ee uhs)* A*, may be a black hole.

The bright areas shown in this image are not created by
visible light, but by X rays given off by Sagittarius A*

Sagittarius A* in an
X-ray image

What Types of Galaxies Are There?

Many **astronomers** agree that there are three basic kinds of **galaxies: spiral** galaxies, **elliptical** galaxies, and irregular galaxies.

Spiral galaxies have arms that are filled with stars. These arms twist around a central point. Spiral galaxies look like pinwheels. The Milky Way (see pages 12 and 13) is a spiral galaxy.

Elliptical galaxies look like clouds of stars. These galaxies vary in shape from near-perfect circles to flattened globes. Elliptical galaxies are brighter at the center than they are at the edges.

Irregular galaxies are some of the strangest looking galaxies. These galaxies can be circular in shape, but they appear to have no distinct pattern of stars. Two irregular galaxies are close enough to the Milky Way to be visible without a telescope. They are called the Large Magellanic Cloud and the Small Magellanic Cloud.

The red-brown, cloudlike features in this elliptical galaxy are formed of cosmic dust

An elliptical galaxy (above) and an irregular galaxy, both in false-color composite photos

Can Galaxies Run into Each Other?

Galaxies are usually very far apart. But sometimes two galaxies get close enough to each other to collide. When this happens, it is not like a car accident in which both cars crash into one another and are smashed up. The stars within the galaxies are so far apart that they do not often run into each other when galaxies collide.

In fact, fast-moving galaxies can sometimes move right through each other with little or no effect at all. If the colliding galaxies are moving slowly, however, the stars in those galaxies may all form one large galaxy—bigger than either of the original galaxies. While the stars in galaxies are far apart, the force of their **gravity** often has the effect of warping, or changing the shape of, both galaxies.

M64—also called
the Black Eye Galaxy—which
scientists believe was made
from two merged galaxies, in
a natural-color photo

The dark shadow at one side of
this galaxy is made up of gas

What Is Special About the Milky Way?

In some ways, it is not very special. The Milky Way actually appears to be pretty ordinary. It is a **spiral galaxy.** It does not look much different from other spiral galaxies.

But there is one thing that is very special about the Milky Way: our **solar system,** which includes the sun and the **planet** Earth, resides there. And, that is special because Earth is the only place that we know has life.

So, the Milky Way is very special to us because it is our home. Overall, though, the Milky Way is just a tiny part of an amazing, complex, and wonderful place called the **universe.**

City lights show populated areas in North and South America

What Is the Universe?

The **universe** is everything. It is all the **matter,** light, and other forms of **energy** that exist, including all the stars, **planets,** and **galaxies.**

The universe is so huge that its size is almost beyond the human imagination. It is so big that scientists think it contains more than 100 billion galaxies. That is just the number of galaxies estimated to exist in the observable universe, or the part of the universe that can be seen from Earth (see page 36). Even traveling at the **speed of light,** it would take billions of years to travel to the most distant galaxies we can see.

During the past 200 years, we have begun to learn how the universe is organized. It is arranged into galaxies, superclusters, and, on a much larger scale, huge stringlike networks of galaxies in space.

Despite the presence of all the stars and galaxies, the vast majority of the universe is almost completely empty of any visible **matter.**

Some of the oldest galaxies in the visible universe, in a false-color composite image

How Old Is the Universe?

Astronomers are not certain about the exact age of the **universe.** Many different kinds of evidence, however, suggest that the universe is about 14 billion years old. Two clues as to the age of the universe are the ages of the stars and the movement of galaxies.

Differences in the **spectrum** of light given off by a star give away the star's chemical make-up. By analyzing the chemical make-up of a star, astronomers can determine a star's age. The oldest stars appear to be about 13 billion years old. It probably took some time before conditions in the early universe were right for stars to form. This suggests the universe began about 14 billion years ago.

More evidence about the age of the universe comes from the movement of the galaxies (see page 40). All faraway galaxies appear to be moving away from one another. Since scientists know how fast the galaxies are separating, they can figure out about how long it has been since these galaxies were all in about the same place. Calculations suggest that the galaxies we can see were bunched extremely close together about 14 billion years ago. Scientists think this tightly packed state produced an explosion called the big bang (see page 42).

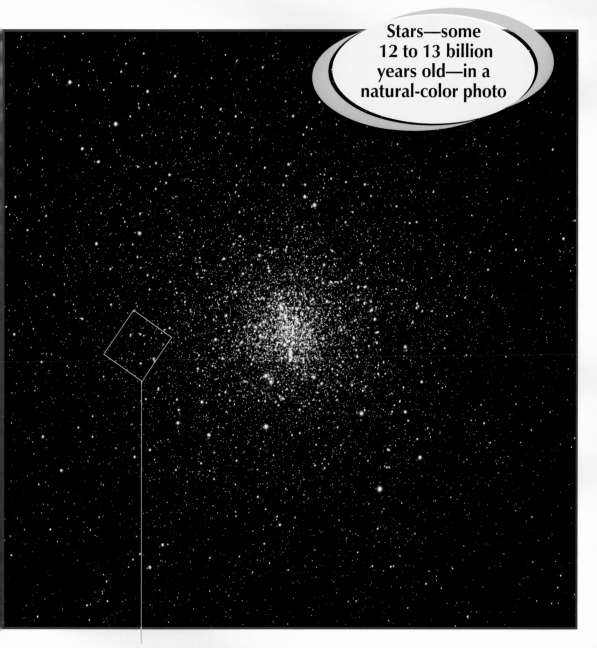

Area in the Milky Way Galaxy containing ancient white-dwarf stars

How Big Is the Universe?

The **universe** is incredibly large. Observations (information gained by watching) made with advanced telescopes indicate that there are at least 100 billion **galaxies** in the observable universe, which is that part of the universe that we can see from Earth. Light, however, takes time to travel, and the universe is only about 14 billion years old. So, there are most likely galaxies farther away whose light has not had enough time to reach us. Evidence suggests that the universe is much larger than what we can see, and it may in fact be infinite (without limits, or unending) in size.

Light reaching Earth from the most distant objects we can see has been traveling for about 12 billion to 13 billion **light-years.** So, by looking at faraway stars and other distant objects, we are actually looking at things as they were long ago.

Galaxies near and distant,
in a false-color photo

Is the Universe Changing?

For a very long time, scientists thought the **universe** never changed. One of the most important scientific discoveries of the 20th century occurred when scientists learned that the universe is actually expanding, or moving outward. Space is getting bigger all the time.

Scientists did not know that there were galaxies other than the Milky Way until 1924. At that time, an American **astronomer** named Edwin Hubble (1889-1953) studied a faint patch of light in the sky. Hubble was able to show that the light was actually a large group of stars that was two million **light-years** away—much farther away than the stars in our **galaxy.** Hubble's work proved that there were other galaxies beyond the Milky Way.

Gravity causes galaxies within the same cluster to stay close together and even at times to collide. When Hubble examined the light from other distant galaxies, however, he found that those galaxies that were far from each other were growing even farther apart. In fact, the farther two galaxies are from each other, the faster the distance between them grows. To astronomers, this finding meant that the entire universe is expanding.

Edwin Hubble looking through the eyepiece of a telescope

How Do Galaxies Move as Space Expands?

All of the **galaxies** that **astronomers** can see, except the very close ones, are moving away from us and from each other at an equal rate. It is not the case, however, that galaxies are moving further from each other *through* space. In reality, as the space within the universe expands, the universe carries the galaxies along *with* it. The galaxies are moving *with* space, not *through* it.

You could compare this to raisin-bread dough. The raisins are the galaxies and the universe is the dough. As shown in the three illustrations below, the dough rises. When it does, the raisins that are embedded within are carried along. This compares with the universe. As space expands, the galaxies contained in space move farther and farther apart.

The spiral galaxy NGC 4414

This galaxy was one used by astronomers to help calculate the rate of the expansion of the universe

What Was the Big Bang?

Most scientists think that the **universe** began expanding in a sudden, violent explosion called the big bang. Scientists consider the big bang to mark the "birth" of our universe. They think the big bang occurred about 14 billion years ago (see page 34).

Similar to when a firecracker explodes, the universe was very hot in the moments after the big bang. As space expanded (stretched), the universe began to cool off. Eventually the universe was cool enough for **matter** to form into stars and **galaxies.** There are differences between the big bang and a usual explosion, however. When a firecracker explodes, the matter and force pushes away from the center of the firecracker. The big bang, however, happened throughout the entire universe, pushing everything away from everything else. There is no center to the big bang.

There is a lot of evidence to support the big bang theory. Using very complicated **instruments, astronomers** have detected small amounts of **energy** in space. Astronomers believe this energy to be left over from the big bang. Called cosmic microwave background radiation, this energy provides the best proof we have that the universe began with a big bang.

The colors in this map represent differences in the temperature of the universe. These differences emerged about 400,000 years after the universe started.

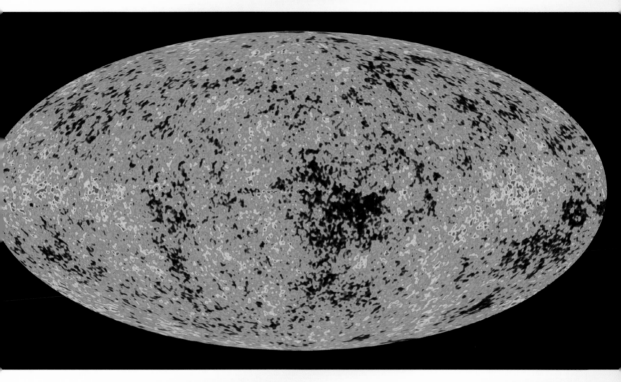

A map of the cosmic microwave background radiation, based on data sent from a probe in 2003

Has the Rate of the Universe's Expansion Sped Up?

The **universe** has continued to expand since the big bang. Scientists once thought that **gravity** was slowing the expansion.

In 1998, however, **astronomers** announced that the **supernovae** in distant **galaxies** appeared dimmer than expected. The brightness of these exploding stars depends on their distance, with closer supernovae appearing brighter. Scientists concluded that the dimmer supernovae were farther away than they should be if the expansion of the universe was slowing up. This suggests that the expansion is actually speeding up.

Scientists think this speeding up involves a mysterious type of **energy** called **dark energy.** Very little is known about dark energy, because it cannot be seen with telescopes or other **instruments.** Dark energy appears to work against the pull of gravity, causing the universe to expand faster and faster.

n 1995, the Hubble Space Telescope aptured this image.

In 2002, the Hubble Space Telescope captured this image. The arrow points to a supernova that is exploding. NASA is using this and other supernovae to measure the rate at which the expansion of the universe is speeding up or slowing down.

A supernova exploding (right), captured in a false-color photo

How Have We Learned So Much About the Universe?

We have learned so much by asking questions! Since ancient times, humans have tried to make sense of the world. The ancient Greeks were among the first people to use science and mathematics to explain how the natural world works. They mapped the stars and measured the size of Earth with surprising accuracy.

As time went on, people learned how to make **instruments** to help them learn about things like the sun, Earth's moon, and the **planets.** For example, most of the great discoveries about how the **universe** is organized occurred because of the invention of complex telescopes.

Today, scientists can send large telescopes into space. One such telescope in space belongs to the United States National Aeronautics and Space Administration (NASA). NASA's Hubble Space Telescope has been able to look farther and more clearly into the universe than anything else that humans have ever made! The Hubble is named for **astronomer** Edwin Hubble (see pages 38 and 39).

The Hubble Space
Telescope

What Kinds of Instruments Do Astronomers Use?

Scientists must use different **instruments** to learn things about the different types of **matter** and **energy** in the **universe.** For example, there is so much dust and gas at the center of the Milky Way that scientists cannot see what the central part of the **galaxy** looks like with telescopes that can see only visible light. But many objects give off other types of **electromagnetic energy** besides visible light, and telescopes can be designed to detect these signals too.

Some stars and other objects give off X rays. By using a type of telescope that can detect these X rays, scientists can "see" through these dust clouds and get an idea of what the center of the galaxy looks like. In addition to X-ray telescopes, scientists also use infrared telescopes and radio telescopes. The latter can detect radio waves given off by distant objects. Although these telescopes detect energy that humans cannot see, they usually turn these signals into images that scientists can understand.

A region of space captured by Hubble
in a false-color image

The same region of
space captured by the
Hubble Space Telescope
and the Chandra X-ray
Observatory

A region of space captured by Chandra
in an X-ray image

What Is Dark Matter?

Dark matter is a substance that scientists think makes up most of the matter in the **universe.** Dark matter is not the same as a black hole (see page 52).

Using the technology we have today, it is very difficult to detect dark matter. That is because dark matter does not shine like stars. It also does not give off radio waves, X rays, or any other type of **electromagnetic energy** that we can detect.

Dark matter cannot be seen directly with telescopes or other **instruments,** but scientists can observe the effects of its **gravity.** For instance, **galaxies** have much more gravity than can be explained by the stars and other **matter** that we can see. Because gravity is dependent on the amount of **mass** that an object has, there must be more matter creating the mass in these galaxies than that which we are able to see or measure.

Dark matter is shown in purple

What Are Black Holes?

Black holes are places in space where **gravity** is so strong that even light, which moves very fast, cannot escape. Black holes are not the same as **dark matter** (see page 50).

Scientists have learned that black holes form when stars much larger than our sun run out of fuel to burn. When this happens, the star collapses under its own gravity until all of its **mass** is concentrated in a tiny space, creating a black hole.

Scientists cannot see black holes with telescopes. However, they think black holes exist because they can see **matter** and **energy** that is being drawn into them by the strong gravity of the black hole. Most **astronomers** think there are millions of small black holes in the Milky Way. They have also found evidence that there may be a very powerful black hole at the center of the Milky Way and other **galaxies.**

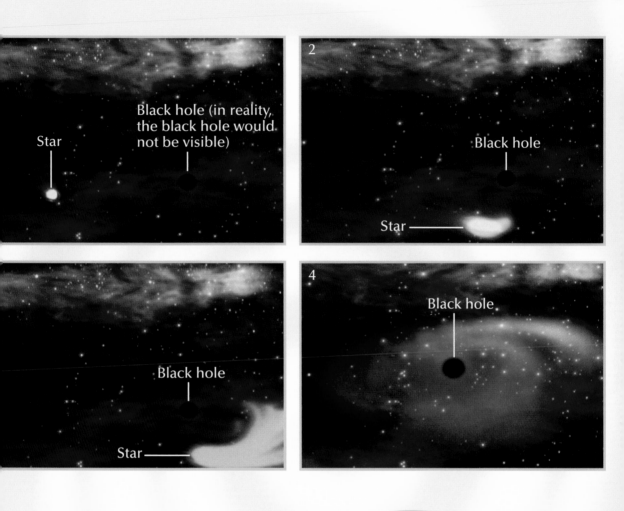

A series of artist's conceptions showing a star being drawn into a black hole

What Are Star Clusters?

Star clusters are large groups of stars that are found within or surrounding a **galaxy.** The clusters exist because the stars are held together by the **gravity** that attracts them to each other.

There are two types of star clusters: open clusters and globular clusters. Open clusters are loose groups of stars that are usually near large clouds of gas and dust. The stars in open clusters are relatively young stars.

Globular clusters are groups of stars that are much closer together than open clusters. Globular clusters are usually larger than open clusters. Scientists think the stars in globular clusters are very old. Some might be as old as 12 billion years. This would make them some of the oldest known stars.

A globular cluster in a false-color photo

What Are Pulsars?

Pulsars are objects in space that give off a strong beam of radio waves—a form of **electromagnetic energy.** Scientists think pulsars are objects left over when large stars run out of fuel to burn. These large stars are not massive enough to form black holes, so when they run out of fuel they explode violently, leaving a small, very dense object called a **neutron star.** Neutrons are particles of **matter** smaller than an atom.

These neutron stars are called "pulsars" because the **energy** they give off appears to come in bursts, or pulses. This is because the pulsar gives off a narrow beam of radio waves that moves as the star spins. We see a "pulse" every time the beam sweeps over Earth.

Pulsars spin very fast. The average pulsar spins twice every second.

A pulsar in an
X-ray image

Could Life Exist Elsewhere in the Universe?

The **universe** is so huge it is almost beyond our imagination. There are certainly plenty of places life could begin. There are at least 100 billion **galaxies** in the observable universe. These galaxies contain trillions (a million million) of stars. Also, scientists continue to discover **planets** circling distant stars.

In the Milky Way alone, there are probably billions of stars that are the right size and temperature to allow life to evolve on planets in **orbit** around them. Scientists do not know for sure, but it is possible that life could arise somewhere else in the universe.

But for now, we have only found life in one place: Earth.

The vastness of space
shown in a
false-color photo

How Will the Universe End?

This is a very difficult question. The answer depends on the relationship among normal **matter, dark matter,** and **dark energy** in the **universe.** It also depends on the nature of dark energy, which is not yet understood.

Evidence suggests that the universe does not have enough normal matter and dark matter for **gravity** to overcome the dark energy that scientists think is responsible for the expansion of the universe. If this is the case, the universe will continue to expand forever until it is so old that all the stars burn out and fade away.

But, should the universe have enough matter, the force of gravity will eventually overcome the dark energy. As a result, the universe will eventually stop expanding and start shrinking. This shrinking will speed up until all the matter in the universe is in a single, tiny space. Scientists call this the "big crunch." However, observations strongly suggest this will not occur.

No matter which of these theories is correct, do not worry. Scientists think the universe will be around for billions of years.

Young stars in the Small Magellanic Cloud in a natural-color photomosaic (incomplete at upper right and lower left corners)

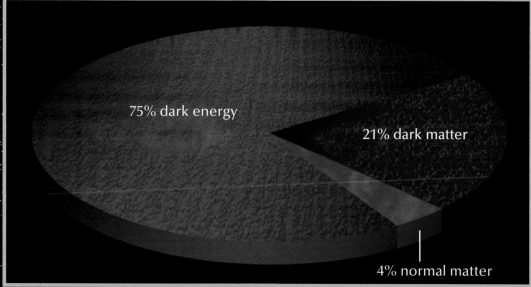

A pie chart showing the amount of matter and energy that some scientists believe exists in the universe

FUN FACTS About GALAXIES & the UNIVERSE

⭐ Only three **galaxies** outside of the Milky Way can easily be seen in a dark sky by the unaided eye here on Earth: the Andromeda Galaxy, which can be seen from the Northern Hemisphere, and the Large Magellanic Cloud and Small Magellanic Cloud, which are visible from the Southern Hemisphere.

⭐ The Milky Way Galaxy rotates around an object called Sagittarius A*, which gives off powerful amounts of radiation. Scientists think this radiation might be given off by a black hole a million times as massive as the sun.

⭐ In 1995, NASA's Hubble Space Telescope took a picture of a tiny area of space very far away and found hundreds of ancient galaxies where scientists thought there would be empty space. Some of these galaxies are as far as 12 to 13 billion **light-years** away.

⭐ Scientists think the big bang happened around 14 billion years ago. To get an idea of the timeline of the **universe**—if we squeezed all the events in the history of the universe into 24 hours, Earth would form in the late afternoon of that 24-hour period, and humans would have existed for only 2 seconds.

⭐ Some scientists think that the universe may begin to expand so fast that galaxies will begin to split apart. This theory is called the "big rip."

Glossary

asteroid A small body made of rock, carbon, or metal that orbits the sun. Most asteroids are between the orbits of Mars and Jupiter.

astronomer A scientist who studies stars and planets.

comet A small body made of dirt and ice that orbits the sun.

dark energy A form of energy that apparently causes the universe to expand more and more rapidly.

dark matter The invisible substance that makes up most of the matter in the universe. Dark matter does not give off visible light, radio waves, X rays, or any other kind of electromagnetic energy. Astronomers know about dark matter only because of its effect on gravity.

electromagnetic energy Energy formed of waves created by the back and forth motion (oscillation) of electric charges. These waves travel through space at the speed of light, which is about 186,282 miles (299,792 kilometers) per second. From longest to shortest, the rays in the electromagnetic spectrum are radio waves, microwaves, infrared rays, visible light, ultraviolet rays, X rays, and gamma rays.

elliptical Having the shape of an ellipse, which is like an oval or flattened circle.

energy A quantity related to work, such as moving an object or an object's giving off heat or light. Light, heat, and electricity are just some of the different forms of energy.

galaxy A group of billions of stars forming one system.

gas giant Any of four planets—Jupiter, Saturn, Uranus, and Neptune—made up mostly of gas and liquid.

gravity The effect of a force of attraction that acts between all objects because of their mass (that is, the amount of matter the objects have).

instrument Machines that measure and record such things as temperature or time.

light-year The distance that light travels in a vacuum (empty space) in one year, equal to about 5.88 trillion miles (9.46 trillion kilometers). A jetliner traveling at a speed of 500 miles (800 kilometers) per hour would need to fly for 1.34 million years in order to travel one light-year.

mass The amount of matter a thing contains.

matter The substance, or material, of which all objects are made.

neutron star The smallest and densest type of star known. These stars give off powerful radio waves and X rays.

nuclear fusion reaction A process that produces energy in the sun's core in which two atomic nuclei (centers) join to create a new, larger nucleus.

orbit The path that a smaller body takes around a larger body, for instance, the path that a planet takes around the sun. Also, to travel in an orbit.

planet A large, round body in space that orbits a star. A planet must have sufficient gravitational pull to clear other objects from the area of its orbit.

pulsar An object in space that gives off regular bursts of electromagnetic radiation. Most of this radiation is in the form of radio waves. Pulsars received their name from these highly regular pulses. Scientists believe pulsars are actually neutron stars.

satellite An artificial satellite is an object built by people and launched into space, where it continuously orbits Earth or some other body.

solar system A group of bodies in space made up of a star and the planets and other objects orbiting around that star.

spectrum A band of visible light, or some other kind of radiation, arranged in order of wavelength. (Wavelength is the distance between successive wave crests.) A rainbow is a spectrum.

speed of light The rate at which light travels, which is 186,282 miles (299,792 kilometers) per second.

spiral A winding and gradually widening curve or coil.

supernova An exploding star.

universe Everything that exists anywhere in space and time.

Index

For more information about galaxies and the universe, try these resources:

*Big Bang! The Tongue-Tickling Tale of a Speck That
    Became Spectacular,* by Carolyn Cinami Decristofano,
    Charlesbridge Publishing, 2005

Galaxies, by Seymour Simon, Sagebrush, 1999

Night Wonders, by Jane Ann Peddicord, Charlesbridge
    Publishing, 2005

The Universe, by Seymour Simon, Sagebrush, 2001

http://imagine.gsfc.nasa.gov/index.html

http://origins.jpl.nasa.gov/library/poster/poster.html

http://starchild.gsfc.nasa.gov/docs/StarChild/StarChild.html

http://www.nasa.gov/vision/universe/starsgalaxies/